Beginning History

THE GUNPOWDER PLOT

Liz Gogerly

Illustrated by Donald Harley

HODDER
Wayland

an imprint of Hodder Children's Books

Text copyright © 2002 Hodder Wayland
Illustrations copyright © 2002 Donald Harley

Project manager: Louisa Sladen
Designer: Peta Morey

First published in 2002 by Hodder Wayland,
an imprint of Hodder Children's Books

This edition published in 2003.

British Library Cataloguing in Publication Data
Gogerly, Liz
The Gunpowder Plot. - (Beginning History)
1. Gunpowder Plot, 1605 - Juvenile literature
I. Title
941'.061

ISBN 0 7502 3793 7

Printed and bound in Hong Kong

Hodder Children's Books
A division of Hodder Headline Limited
338 Euston Road, London NW1 3BH

Picture Acknowledgements
The publishers would like to thank the following for allowing their pictures to be
reproduced in this publication: Ashmolean Museum/Bridgeman Art Library *back
cover*; Private Collection/Bridgeman Art Library 4, 5, 15; Longleat House,
Wiltshire/Bridgeman Art Library 9; Mary Evans Picture Library 7, 10, 21; National
Portrait Gallery 10; Hodder Wayland Picture Library *title page*, 3, 6 (top and
bottom), 12, 16, 18 (top and bottom), 19; National Trust Photographic Library 8;
The Fotomas Index 14; Peter Newark Picture Library 11;
Chistine Nesbitt/Reuters/Popperfoto 20.

While every effort has been made to secure permission, in some cases it has
proved impossible to trace copyright holders.

Contents

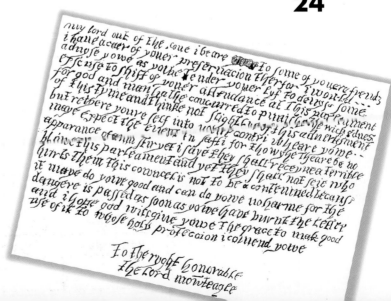

The Truth About Bonfire Night

On 5 November every year, children get excited because it's Bonfire Night or Guy Fawkes' Night. We enjoy fireworks. We watch as bonfires burn in the cold night air. We cheer as the guy on top of the fire is set alight.

Children wave sparklers, and colourful fireworks light up the sky on Bonfire Night.
▼

These Victorian children have made a guy. Just like children do today, they shout, 'Penny for the guy?' in the hope that people will give them money.

Guy Fawkes was tall, with reddish-brown hair and a moustache. Dressed in his soldier's uniform, he looked strong and powerful.

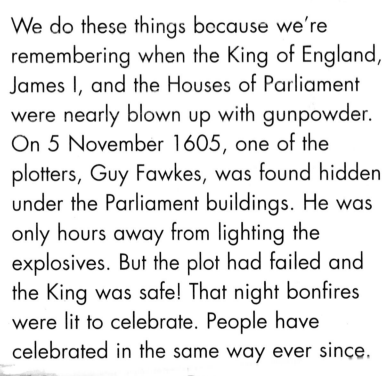

We do these things because we're remembering when the King of England, James I, and the Houses of Parliament were nearly blown up with gunpowder. On 5 November 1605, one of the plotters, Guy Fawkes, was found hidden under the Parliament buildings. He was only hours away from lighting the explosives. But the plot had failed and the King was safe! That night bonfires were lit to celebrate. People have celebrated in the same way ever since.

Catholics and Protestants

This is a painting of King Henry VIII by Hans Holbein. Holbein became the portrait painter at the King's court.
▼

Nearly five hundred years ago, religion was an important part of everyone's life. Most people in England were Catholics. This changed during the reign of King Henry VIII. When he made himself the head of the Church of England in 1532, his followers became Protestants. Catholic churches were sold and Catholics were killed. There would be violent arguments between Protestants and Catholics for many years to come.

◄ This is a portrait of Henry VIII's second wife, Anne Boleyn. Henry VIII left the Catholic Church in order to marry her.

Henry VIII's son, who became King Edward VI in 1547, was a Protestant also. But, in 1553, when his Catholic half sister became Queen Mary I, she punished Protestants. Everything changed again when Queen Elizabeth I ascended the throne in 1558. As a Protestant, she passed laws against the Catholics. Guy Fawkes was born into a Catholic family during her reign.

While Queen Mary I ruled, over 300 Protestants were put to death. Ordinary people, as well as bishops, were burned for their beliefs.

Who was Guy Fawkes?

Guy Fawkes was born in York, in 1570. We don't know the exact day he was born, but he was baptized on 16 April 1570. At school, his teacher and many of his friends were Catholic. Like other Catholics, they had to practise their religion in secret. There were fines for people who didn't attend the Protestant church on Sunday or on holy days. And, for Catholic priests caught holding their church service, the punishment was death.

Many big houses in England owned by Catholic families contained hidden rooms known as priest holes. Priests could hold the Catholic service secretly in these places.

Like many other Catholic families, the Cobhams were rich and well thought of in society. They still had to keep their religion secret though.

▼

▲ Guy plays marbles with his school friends. Three of his friends grew up to become Catholic priests and were put to death during the reign of Queen Elizabeth I.

As he grew older, Guy became angry about the way Catholics were treated. In the 1590s he left England for Spain, a Catholic country. While he was there he became a soldier fighting for the Spanish. He was famous for being brave – and he learned how to use gunpowder...

A Plot to Kill the King

In 1603, Queen Elizabeth I died. She had chosen King James VI of Scotland as her successor. He became King James I of England. James I was young and intelligent but he was also a Protestant. He passed more laws against the Catholics. Their lives were more dangerous than ever.

▲ Although King James I's mother, Mary Queen of Scots, was a Catholic, her son didn't share her beliefs.

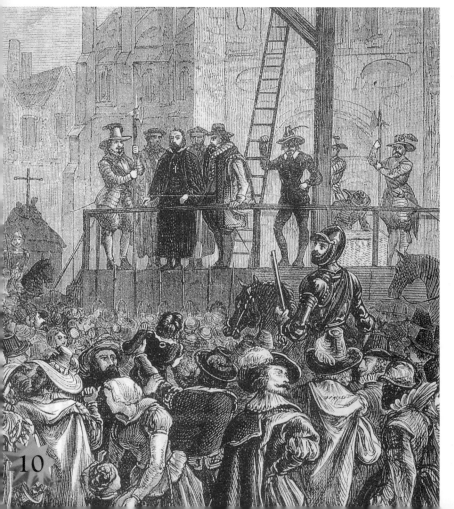

◄ The priest in this picture is about to be hanged. Many Catholic priests were put to death during King James I's reign.

Guy Fawkes wanted to stop the punishment of Catholics in England. While he was in Spain, he met a Catholic called Thomas Winter. Thomas told Guy about his plan. It was to blow up both King James I and the Houses of Parliament, where the laws that governed England were made. It was a dangerous plot but Guy wanted to be part of it.

▲ In 1605, the Houses of Parliament were made up of many small buildings. Next to these buildings were private houses, shops and inns. It was a busy area and it was easy for the plotters not to be seen.

11

The Secret Meeting

When Guy returned to England he had to be careful. Now he was involved in the gunpowder plot, he had to live a secret life. Meetings were held in dark and smoky inns. On 20 May 1604, he met the rest of the plotters in the Duck and Drake Inn in London.

Guy Fawkes with seven of the other plotters. Can you spot the two pairs of brothers in the picture?

▼

Robert Catesby was the leader of the gang. He was joined by Thomas Winter, and two of Guy Fawkes' old school friends, Jack Wright and Thomas Percy. Robert was a strong and handsome leader. The men listened carefully to him.

Over a Bible, Guy Fawkes, Robert Catesby, Thomas Winter, Jack Wright and Thomas Percy swear to keep the plot a secret.

▼

The Plot Unfolds

Robert Catesby's plot was simple – the next time Parliament was opened by King James I, they would blow up everyone there with gunpowder.

▲ **King James I sits before the Members of Parliament. In those days, Parliament could only meet with the King's permission.**

14

With the King and the Members of Parliament dead, the plotters could put James I's daughter, Princess Elizabeth, on the throne. She was just nine years old, but soon she would be made to marry a Catholic Spanish prince. England would be a Catholic nation again! Excited by their plan, the plotters swore to keep their secret.

The plotters decided that Guy Fawkes should stay in London. He took a false name, and looked for a house to rent near to the Houses of Parliament. At last, the plot was moving forward!

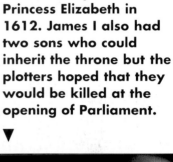

The sixteen-year-old Princess Elizabeth in 1612. James I also had two sons who could inherit the throne but the plotters hoped that they would be killed at the opening of Parliament.

▼

Set to Explode!

In those days the Houses of Parliament were just a few small buildings. The plotters rented a house next door. The house was perfect for their plan. It had a cellar that led underneath the Parliament buildings. The cellar had been used to store wood and coal. Barrels of gunpowder could be easily hidden in this dark, untidy place.

◀ At night, Guy Fawkes and Robert Catesby made secret boat trips across the Thames with the barrels of gunpowder, taking them to their hiding place.

▲ Thirty-six barrels of gunpowder were hidden in the cellars. Guy had to take care – a single spark from a flame would cause an explosion!

By the autumn of 1605, there were thirteen men involved in the plot. But Guy Fawkes lived in the house by himself. It was his job to look after the gunpowder. When the time came, he was to light the fuse that would make the gunpowder explode.

Caught in the Act

The opening of Parliament was planned for the end of October 1605. The gunpowder was in place. Guy Fawkes was waiting for the right moment to light the fuse. Everything seemed to be going well, but the plotters didn't know that news of the plot had leaked out.

On 26 October 1605, a secret letter was sent to Catholic Lord Monteagle. In the letter was a warning not to attend the opening of Parliament. Lord Monteagle decided he must show the letter to King James I.

Lord Monteagle receives the mysterious letter warning of the Gunpowder Plot. As a reward for warning the King, Lord Monteagle was given land and money.

▼

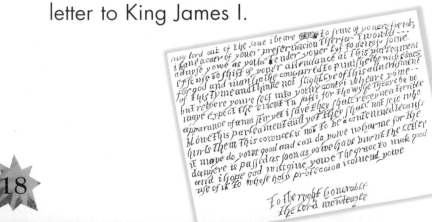

◄ Who wrote the letter to Lord Monteagle? Did one of the plotters break their promise and warn a family member or friend who might have been in danger? We will probably never know the truth.

A few days later, the King ordered that the buildings next to the Houses of Parliament be searched. On the morning of 5 November, soldiers discovered Guy hidden in the cellar and arrested him. The trail of gunpowder at his feet would never be lit.

The King's men made two searches of the Houses of Parliament before they found Guy Fawkes. When they heard about Guy's arrest the other plotters left London and went into hiding.

▼

Gunpowder, Treason and Plot...

Guy Fawkes was taken to the Tower of London. Soldiers tried to get him to admit his crime. He was tortured and questioned about the other plotters. To start with he didn't tell the soldiers anything about the plot. But, eventually, he started to tell the truth.

Each year, at the State Opening of Parliament, the Yeoman of the Guard search the cellars of the Houses of Parliament. This is done in the memory of the Gunpowder Plot.

▼

Robert Catesby and the other men stayed in hiding until they were discovered in Holbeach House in Worcestershire. Four men were shot dead, including Robert Catesby and Thomas Percy. In January 1606, Guy and the other gang members were sentenced to a traitor's death and executed. It was a horrible way to die. But Guy Fawkes died believing in everything he'd done. And no one in England would ever forget him!

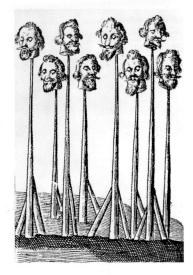

▲ The heads of the traitors were displayed in public in London. It was a horrible reminder that plotting against the King was punishable by death!

Remember, remember, the fifth of November,
Gunpowder, Treason and Plot,
We know no reason why Gunpowder Treason
Should ever be forgot.

Glossary

Ascended To have moved upwards, or, to have taken on a higher role, such as that of a king or queen.

Baptized To have poured water on a baby's head as a sign that he or she is a Christian.

Catholics People who believe that the Pope in Rome is the head of their religion.

Celebrate To enjoy a special occasion.

Cellar A room, usually below the ground level of a house, where things can be stored.

Fuse The string attached to the gunpowder. It is lit to make the gunpowder explode.

Governed To have made laws and controlled a country or place.

Gunpowder A powder which explodes easily when it's set alight.

Holy days Days when we celebrate religious events. On Christmas Day we celebrate the birth of Christ.

Laws Rules made by Members of Parliament or the government. People who break these rules are punished.

Plotters A group of people who make a secret plan together.

Priest The person who leads the services and ceremonies in the Catholic church.

Protestants People who believe that the king or queen is the head of the Church of England.

Reign The period of time that a king or queen spends as monarch of their country.

Successor The person who takes over the job or role of another person.

Tortured To have hurt and punished someone.

Traitor Someone who turns against his or her country and its ruler.

Treason A crime against a country or its ruler.

Further Information

Books to Read

Guy Fawkes (in the Life Stories series) by Clare Chandler (Hodder Wayland,1998)
Guy Fawkes (in the Life and Times series) by Rachael Bell (Heinemann, 2000)
Gunpowder Guy (in the Stories From History series) by Stewart Ross (Hodder Wayland, 2000)

Websites You Can Visit

Read all about the Gunpowder Plot, enjoy a visit to an Elizabethan fashion show, find out what Guy Fawkes ate and listen to Elizabethan music. Finally, try the special quiz to test how much you know about the Gunpowder Plot!
www.bcpl.net/~cbladey/ guy/html/menu1.html

Tour the famous Tower of London where Guy Fawkes was tortured. With music and fireworks this site brings the past alive.
www.toweroflondontour. com/kids/queen.html

Places to Visit

Palace of Westminster, London SW1 – you can look at the outside of the new Palace of Westminster and the Houses of Parliament – tours of the inside are by special arrangement only!

The Tower of London, Tower Hill, London EC3 (Telephone: 020 7709 0765) – you can visit the Tower of London where Guy Fawkes and other traitors in history were tortured.

York Dungeon, 12 Clifford Street, York YO1 IRD (Telephone: 01904 632599) – you can relive the Gunpowder Plot in the Guy Fawkes Experience.

Index